CRAZY IDIOMS

CRAZY
IDIOMS

A
CONVERSATIONAL
IDIOM
BOOK

NINA WEINSTEIN

COLLIER
MACMILLAN

Editors: Mary Jane Peluso/ Maggie Barbieri
Production supervision: Cristina Escobar/ Publication Services
Cover design: Deborah Barnett-Brandt/ Angie Kimball
Illustrations: Don Robb

This book was set in 13/15 Stone Serif by Publication Services, printed and bound by Quinn-Woodbine Inc. The cover was printed by Lehigh Press Lithographers.

Collier Macmillan Canada, Inc.

LIBRARY OF CONGRESS CATALOGING-IN-PUBLICATION DATA

Weinstein, Nina J.
     Crazy idioms: a conversational idiom book/ Nina Weinstein.
     p. cm.
     Includes index.
     ISBN 0-02-425361-8
     1. English language—Textbooks for foreign speakers.   2. English language—Conversation and phrase books.   3. English language––Idioms.   I. Title.
     PE1128.W4255 1990   89-7298
     428.3'4—dc20   CIP

Printing: 1 2 3 4 5 6 7   Year: 0 1 2 3 4 5 6
Collier Macmillan
ESL/EFL Department
866 Third Avenue
New York, NY 10022

Printed in the U.S.A.
ISBN 0-02-425361-8

Introduction

Crazy Idioms is a very basic, short course on idioms that's a lot of fun and can be learned in a few weeks. Because it's easier to remember idioms that have something in common, the forty-five idioms in *Crazy Idioms* are divided into the following categories: **Animal Idioms, Food Idioms, Color Idioms, Body Idioms**, and **Dangerous Idioms** (idioms with double meanings).

The exercises are simple and fun. Each unit ends with a "Use What You Learned" section that gives students practice in using the idioms in semifree conversation. Everyone in the class gets up from his or her seat. Then students are told to find someone who, for example, "eats like a bird." They must ask everyone in the class "Do you eat like a bird?" until they find someone who says "Yes." That person signs his or her name in the space provided. There are several questions of this type, and it's expected that students will do each question at a different pace so that the atmosphere in the classroom becomes like a party. The teacher is free to walk around the classroom and supervise those who need it.

Crazy Idioms comes with an audiocassette.

Contents

CRAZY IDIOMS

UNIT 1
ANIMAL IDIOMS, PART 1

Idiom Preview

Can you guess what these idioms mean?

- ☐ to eat like a horse

- ☐ to be chicken

- ☐ to run around like a chicken with its head cut off

- ☐ to eat like a bird

- ☐ to quit something cold turkey

Moving Day

☺☺ *Carlos is helping Juan move into his new apartment.*

Carlos: Do you have a cigarette?

Juan: I thought you quit **cold turkey**.

Carlos: I did, but I started again. *(He looks at his watch.)* It's lunchtime. Do you have anything to eat?

Juan: Only half a sandwich.

Carlos: That won't be enough. **I eat like a horse**. You take it. You **eat like a bird**.

Juan: **I'm chicken**. It's been in the refrigerator for six weeks. I haven't had time to go shopping. Ever since I found this apartment, I've been **running around like a chicken with its head cut off**.

Matching Idioms

Work with a partner. Match each idiom with the correct picture.

____   1. to eat like a bird

____   2. to eat like a horse

____   3. to quit (something)
           cold turkey

____   4. to run around like a
           chicken with its
           head cut off

____   5. to be chicken

Comparison

Work with a partner. Discuss the following questions.

1. "To eat like a bird" means to eat small amounts of food. Does "to eat like a bird" mean the same thing in your native language?

2. "To eat like a horse" means to eat large amounts of food. Does it mean the same thing in your native language?

3. "To be chicken" means to be afraid. Do you have any idioms with the word "chicken" in your native language?

4. "To run around like a chicken with its head cut off" means to be so busy, you feel completely disorganized. What idiom means the same thing in your native language?

5. "To quit (something) cold turkey" means to stop a bad habit suddenly. What expression means the same thing in your native language?

Use What You Learned

Get up from your seat. Find a person in your class who:

1. feels that he's/she's running around like a chicken with its head cut off.

   _____
   (Name of student)

   Example: You must ask "Do you feel like you're running around like a chicken with its head cut off?" until you find someone who says "Yes." Then ask that person to sign his/her name in the space.

2. eats like a bird.

   _____
   (Name of student)

3. eats like a horse.

   _____
   (Name of student)

4 has quit a bad habit cold turkey.

   _____
   (Name of student)

5. is chicken to fly in an airplane.

   _____
   (Name of student)

UNIT 2
ANIMAL IDIOMS,
PART 2

Idiom Preview

Can you guess what these idioms mean?

- [ ] to work like a dog

- [ ] to be foxy

- [ ] to eat like a pig

- [ ] to be a rat

- [ ] to be a turkey

Politicians

Kim and Andre are talking about politicians.

Kim: Who do you think would be the best governor?

Andre: Well, one of them is a **turkey**, and the other is a **rat**.

Kim: I like the young one. He's really **foxy**.

Andre: But he **eats like a pig**.

Kim: No one's perfect. Anyway, he **works like a dog**. We need someone like that.

Matching Idioms

Work with a partner. Match each idiom with the correct picture.

_____ 1. to eat like a pig

_____ 2. to work like a dog

_____ 3. to be foxy

_____ 4. to be a turkey

_____ 5. to be a rat

Comparison

Work with a partner. Discuss the following questions.

1. "To be a turkey" means to be a jerk, a stupid person. Does it mean the same thing in your native language?

2. "To be a rat" means to be a bad person; someone who does mean things to other people. Do you have any idioms with the word "rat" in your native language?

3. "To be foxy" means to be sexy. Does it mean the same thing in your native language?

4. "To work like a dog" means to work really hard. What expression means the same thing in your native language?

5. "To eat like a pig" means to have bad table manners. Does it mean the same thing in your native language?

Use What You Learned

Get up from your seat. Find a person in your class who:

1. thinks he/she works like a dog.

    _____
    (Name of student)

    Example: You must ask "Do you think you work like a dog?"
    until you find someone who says "Yes." Then ask that person
    to sign his/her name in the space.

2. knows someone who's a rat.

    _____
    (Name of student)

3. knows someone who eats like a pig.

    _____
    (Name of student)

4. has a friend who's foxy.

    _____
    (Name of student)

5. has a friend who's a turkey.

    _____
    (Name of student)

UNIT 3
FOOD IDIOMS,
PART 1

Idiom Preview

Can you guess what these idioms mean?

- to be cool as a cucumber

- to be the top banana

- to be a peach

- to be a smart cookie

- to be a nut/to be nutty

Workers

☺☺ *Mohammed and Lisa are talking on the telephone.*

Mohammed: Did Sandra get her raise yet?

Lisa: No, but she's **cool as a cucumber.**

Mohammed: Well, she's **the top banana**. She has nothing to worry about.

Lisa: Yeah, she's **a peach**.

Mohammed: She's also **a very smart cookie.** She helped the company save lots of money. But I've helped the company, too.

Lisa: Oh? How?

Mohammed: I've helped them spend the money that Sandra saved.

Lisa: You're **a real nut**.

Matching Idioms

Work with a partner. Match each idiom with the correct picture.

_____ 1. to be cool as a
cucumber

a.

_____ 2. to be a peach

b.

_____ 3. to be the top
banana

c.

_____ 4. to be a smart
cookie

d.

_____ 5. to be a nut/
to be nutty

e.

Comparison

Work with a partner. Discuss the following questions.

1. "To be cool as a cucumber" means to be very calm. Do you
   have any expressions with "cucumber" in your native
   language?

2. "To be a peach" means to be a very nice person. What
   expression means the same thing in your native language?

3. "To be the top banana" means to be the most important
   person in a group. Do you have any expressions with
   "banana" in your native language?

4. "To be a smart cookie" means to be intelligent. Does it mean
   the same thing in your native language?

5. "To be a nut/to be nutty" means to act crazy. What
   expression means the same thing in your native language?

Use What You Learned

Get up from your seat. Find a person in your class who:

1. has a friend who's a peach.

   _____
   (Name of student)

   Example: You must ask "Do you have a friend who's a peach?" until you find someone who says "Yes." Then ask that person to sign his/her name in the space.

2. has a friend who's a nut.

   _____
   (Name of student)

3. sometimes acts nutty.

   _____
   (Name of student)

4. has a friend who's the top banana at school or at work.

   _____
   (Name of student)

5. is usually cool as a cucumber.

   _____
   (Name of student)

6. knows a smart cookie.

  _____
  (Name of student)

7. is a smart cookie.

  _____
  (Name of student)

8. likes cookies.

  _____
  (Name of student)

UNIT 4
FOOD IDIOMS,
PART 2

Idiom Preview

Can you guess what these idioms mean?

- □ to bring home the bacon

- □ to walk on eggshells

- □ to be as easy as pie/to be a piece of cake

- □ to be out to lunch

- □ to be a lemon

The Computer

Kim is telling her friend, Yoshio, what happened at work.

Kim: They bought a new computer at work.

Yoshio: That's great.

Kim: It's **a lemon**. And my parents are having some problems, so they're depending on me **to bring home the bacon**.

Yoshio: Computers **are as easy as pie** to use. Maybe the person who bought the computer can help.

Kim: No. He's **out to lunch.** He can't even turn it on. Could you come over and explain it to me?

Yoshio: Well, my father's in a bad mood. I've been **walking on eggshells** all day. How about tomorrow?

Matching Idioms

Work with a partner. Match each idiom with the correct picture.

____ 1. to be a lemon

a.

____ 2. to bring home the bacon

b.

____ 3. to be as easy as pie/ to be a piece of cake

c.

____ 4. to be out to lunch

d.

____ 5. to walk on eggshells

e.

Comparison

Work with a partner. Discuss the following questions.

1. "To be a lemon" means to be bad, defective. It usually describes something electrical or mechanical (Example: cars, computers, typewriters, washing machines, etc.). What expression means the same thing in your native language?

2. "To bring home the bacon" means to earn the money for food, clothing, rent, and so on. What idiom means the same thing in your native language?

3. "To be as easy as pie/to be a piece of cake" means to be very easy. Do you have any expressions with "pie" or "cake" in your native language?

4. "To be out to lunch" means to be a stupid person, a turkey. Does it mean the same thing in your native language?

5. "To walk on eggshells" means to be extremely careful in what we do or say; too careful. When someone's in a bad mood, we have to walk on eggshells around him or her. What expression means the same thing in your native language?

Use What You Learned

Get up from your seat. Find a person in your class who:

1. thinks learning his/her native language is as easy as pie.

_____
(Name of student)

Example: You must ask "Do you think learning your native language is as easy as pie?" until you find someone who says "Yes." Then ask that person to sign his/her name in the space.

2. thinks learning English is a piece of cake.

_____
(Name of student)

3. brings home the bacon.

_____
(Name of student)

4. has a neighbor who's out to lunch.

_____
(Name of student)

5. bought something that's a lemon.

_____
(Name of student)

6. gave something to someone that's a lemon.

_____
(Name of student)

7. likes people to walk on eggshells around him/her.

_____
(Name of student)

UNIT 5
COLOR IDIOMS,
PART 1

Idiom Preview

Can you guess what these idioms mean?

- ☐ to feel blue

- ☐ to be in the pink

- ☐ once in a blue moon

- ☐ to have a green thumb

- ☐ in the red

The Business

Karen is visiting Linda.

Linda: I **feel blue**.

Karen: Why? Are you sick?

Linda: No. I'm **in the pink**.

Karen: Then, what?

Linda: My new gardening business is **in the red** again.

Karen: Oh, no.

Linda: I might have to close it.

Karen: But you **have a green thumb**. You're perfect for this business. What else would you do?

Linda: I don't know. We only get new customers **once in a blue moon**, so I have to decide soon.

Matching Idioms

Work with a partner. Match each idiom with the correct picture.

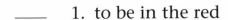

_____ 1. to be in the red   a.

_____ 2. to feel blue   b.

_____ 3. to be in the pink   c.

_____ 4. to have a green thumb   d.

_____ 5. once in a blue moon   e.

Comparison

Work with a partner. Discuss the following questions.

1. "To feel blue" means to feel sad, depressed. What expression means the same thing in your native language?

2. "To be in the red" means to be in debt, to owe more money than you have. Does it mean the same thing in your native language?

3. "To be in the pink" means to be very healthy. What idiom means the same thing in your native language?

4. "To have a green thumb" means to have an ability to make plants grow. What expression means the same thing in your native language?

5. "Once in a blue moon" means very infrequently; hardly ever. Do you have any expressions with "blue" in your native language?

Use What You Learned

Get up from your seat. Find a person in your class who:

1. has a green thumb.

    _____
    (Name of student)

    Example: You must ask "Do you have a green thumb?" until you
    find someone who says "Yes." Than ask that person to sign his/
    her name in the space.

2. feels blue.

    _____
    (Name of student)

3. has a friend who feels blue.

    _____
    (Name of student)

4. is in the pink.

    _____
    (Name of student)

5. writes letters once in a blue moon.

    _____
    (Name of student)

6. receives letters once in a blue moon.

   _____
   (Name of student)

7. is in the red this month.

   _____
   (Name of student)

8. has never been in the red.

   _____
   (Name of student)

UNIT 6
COLOR IDIOMS, PART 2

Idiom Preview

Can you guess what these idioms mean?

- to be white as a sheet

- to be yellow

- to see red

- to be in the black

- to be tickled pink

Balancing the Checkbook

Mohammed and Maria are married.

Mohammed: You look **white as a sheet**.

Maria: I do?

Mohammed: Yes. What's wrong?

Maria: **I'm** too **yellow** to tell you.

Mohammed: Not the checkbook again. I thought we were **in the black**.

Maria: Us? You must be joking.

Mohammed: I **see red** every time you joke about money.

Maria: Well, just wait a minute. *(She adds together some numbers.)* You're going **to be tickled pink**. The checkbook balances for the first time in months!

Matching Idioms

Work with a partner. Match each idiom with the correct picture.

____ 1. to see red

a.

____ 2. to be tickled pink

b.

____ 3. to be in the black

c.

____ 4. to be yellow

d.

____ 5. to be white as a sheet

e.

Color Idioms, Part 2

Comparison

Work with a partner. Discuss the following questions.

1. "To see red" means to be very angry. Do you have any expressions with "red" in your native language?

2. "To be yellow" means to be afraid, to be chicken. What expression means the same thing in your native language?

3. "To be tickled pink" means to be very happy, pleased. What idiom means the same thing in your native language?

4. "To be white as a sheet" means to be very pale in the face because of illness or fear. How do you say the same thing in your native language?

5. "To be in the black" means to have enough money to pay all of your bills. It's the opposite of "to be in the red." Do you have any expressions with "black" in your native language?

Use What You Learned

Get up from your seat. Find a person in your class who:

1. is tickled pink about something.

   _____
   (Name of student)

   Example: You must ask "Are you tickled pink about something?" until you find someone who says "Yes." Then ask that person to sign his/her name in the space.

2. is white as a sheet.

   _____
   (Name of student)

3. has a friend who's yellow.

   _____
   (Name of student)

4. is in the black this month.

   _____
   (Name of student)

5. is in the black every month.

   _____
   (Name of student)

6. sees red every time his/her neighbor plays loud music.

   _____
   (Name of student)

7. becomes white as a sheet when he/she has to take a test.

   _____
   (Name of student)

8. becomes white as a sheet when he/she has to ask someone for a date.

   _____
   (Name of student)

UNIT 7
BODY IDIOMS,
PART 1

Idiom Preview

Can you guess what these idioms mean?

- ☐ to put your foot in your mouth

- ☐ to have a swollen head

- ☐ to lend someone an ear

- ☐ to have your finger in many pies

- ☐ to be tightfisted

Parents

David and Victor are talking about Victor's father.

Victor: I really **put my foot in my mouth** yesterday. I need you **to lend me an ear.**

David: What happened?

Victor: I asked my dad for a new car, and when he said "no," I told him he **was tightfisted.**

David: Do you think he can afford a new car right now?

Victor: He's **got his finger in many pies** at work. But if he cared about me, he'd try.

David: I think you**'ve got a swollen head.** Why don't you buy your own car?

Victor: I never thought of it.

Matching Idioms

Work with a partner. Match each idiom with the correct picture.

____ 1. to put your foot
in your mouth

a.

____ 2. to lend someone
an ear

b.

____ 3. to be tightfisted

c.

____ 4. to have your finger
in many pies

d.

____ 5. to have a swollen
head

e.

Comparison

Work with a partner. Discuss the following questions.

1. "To have a swollen head" means to think you're more important than you really are. Does it mean the same thing in your native language?

2. "To lend someone an ear" means to listen to someone. Do you have any expressions with "ear" in your native language?

3. "To put your foot in your mouth" means to say something accidentally that hurts or bothers someone else. What expression means the same thing in your native language?

4. "To have your finger in many pies" means to be involved in a lot of different projects at the same time. What expression means the same thing in your native language?

5. "To be tightfisted" means to hate to spend money. What idiom means the same thing in your native language?

Use What You Learned

Get up from your seat. Find a person in your class who:

1. sometimes puts his foot in his mouth.

   _____
   (Name of student)

   Example: You must ask "Do you sometimes put your foot in your mouth?" until you find someone who says "Yes." Then ask that person to sign his/her name in the space.

2. often puts their foot in their mouth.

   _____
   (Name of student)

3. knows someone who has a swollen head.

   _____
   (Name of student)

4. is tightfisted.

   _____
   (Name of student)

5. has parents who are tightfisted.

   _____
   (Name of student)

6. has his/her finger in many pies.

    _____
               (Name of student)

7. often lends his/her friend an ear.

    _____
               (Name of student)

8. put their foot in their mouth yesterday.

    _____
               (Name of student)

UNIT 8
BODY IDIOMS,
PART 2

Idiom Preview

Can you guess what these idioms mean?

- ☐ to hold your tongue

- ☐ to be hotheaded

- ☐ to keep your chin up

- ☐ not to have anything between the ears

- ☐ to keep someone at arm's length

Grades

✪ ✪ *Sam is leaving the classroom. He just got his math test back.*

Sam: I didn't pass. My father's very **hotheaded**. He's going to kill me!

Linda: Don't worry about it. You'll do better next time.

Sam: This was the final exam. My father's going to tell me I **don't have anything between the ears.**

Linda: **Keep your chin up**. It's not that bad.

Sam: It's worse. Maybe I can talk to the teacher.

Linda: I'd **hold my tongue** if I were you. You might make it worse.

Sam: You're right. He **keeps everyone at arm's length** anyway. He probably wouldn't listen.

Matching Idioms

Work with a partner. Match each idiom with the correct picture.

____ 1. to hold your tongue

a.

____ 2. to be hotheaded

b.

____ 3. to keep your chin up

c.

____ 4. not to have anything between the ears

d.

____ 5. to keep someone at arm's length

e.

Comparison

Work with a partner. Discuss the following questions.

1. "To hold your tongue" means to keep quiet when you want to say something. Does it mean the same thing in your native language?

2. "To be hotheaded" means to get angry very easily. What expression means the same thing in your native language?

3. "To keep your chin up" means not to show feelings of fear, sadness, and so on, when faced with disappointments, problems, or difficulties. Do you have expressions with "chin" in your native language?

4. "Not to have anything between the ears" means to be stupid. How do you say the same thing in your native language?

5. "To keep someone at arm's length" means to avoid being close or friendly. What expression means the same thing in your native language?

Use What You Learned

Get up from your seat. Find a person in your class who:

1. is sometimes hotheaded.

   _____
   (Name of student)

   Example: You must ask "Are you sometimes hotheaded?" until you find someone who says "Yes." Then ask that person to sign his/her name in the space.

2. has a friend who's hotheaded.

   _____
   (Name of student)

3. often has to hold his/her tongue.

   _____
   (Name of student)

4. believes it's important to keep his/her chin up.

   _____
   (Name of student)

5. has a friend who doesn't have anything between the ears.

   _____
   (Name of student)

6. has lots of friends who don't have anything between the ears.

_____
(Name of student)

7. keeps people at arm's length.

_____
(Name of student)

8. doesn't keep people at arm's length.

_____
(Name of student)

UNIT 9
DANGEROUS
IDIOMS

Not Dangerous		*Dangerous*
	buns	
	to look at one's drawers	
	to run around	
	toilet water	
	to be high	

Misunderstandings

Tom and Vickie are talking about their plans for the weekend.

Tom: I think I'll just stay home. My wife says I **run around** too much.

Vickie: You do?

Tom: No. I mean, yes. I have too many things to do. What about you? What are you going to do?

Vickie: Well, my boyfriend asked me **to look at his drawers**. He's worried about them.

Tom: He is?

Vickie: Well, no. I mean, I fix furniture, and one of his drawers is stuck.

Tom: Oh. Hmm . . . . Yeah, I'll just stay home.

Vickie: Yeah?

Tom: Yeah. I want my wife to try on some **toilet water**.

Vickie: You do?

Tom: Yes. It's our anniversary, and I bought her a small bottle yesterday.

Vickie: Oh.

Tom: I **was** really **high** when I saw it.

Vickie: You were?

Tom: Of course. It was on sale.

Vickie: Oh my gosh! *(She runs out of the room.)*

Tom: What's wrong?

Vickie: My **buns** are burning! I forgot they were in the oven!

Matching Idioms

Work with a partner. Match each idiom with the correct picture.

_____ 1. toilet water

a.

_____ 2. buns

b.

_____ 3. to run around

c.

_____ 4. to look at one's drawers

d.

_____ 5. to be high

e.

Comparison

Work with a partner. Discuss the following questions.

1. "Buns" are the bread used on a hamburger. Does this word mean the same thing in your native language? Does it have any other meanings?

2. "Toilet water" is an inexpensive type of perfume. Does it mean the same thing in your native language?

3. "To run around" means to be very busy doing errands or lots of small jobs. What does it mean in your native language?

4. "To look at one's drawers" means to look at a chest of drawers. What is a chest of drawers called in your native language? Does it have any other meanings?

5. "To be high" means to be very excited about something. What does it mean in your native language? Does it have any other meanings?

Review Test

Now use what you've learned from the entire book. Get up from your seat. Find a person in your class who:

1. quit smoking cold turkey.

   _____
   (Name of student)

   Example: You must ask "Did you quit smoking cold turkey?" until you find someone who says "Yes." Then ask that person to sign his/her name in the space.

2. was running around like a chicken with its head cut off last week.

   _____
   (Name of student)

3. ate like a horse last night.

   _____
   (Name of student)

4. has a brother or sister who eats like a pig.

   _____
   (Name of student)

5. has a brother or sister who eats like a bird.

   _____
   (Name of student)

6. is chicken to cut his/her hair.

_____
(Name of student)

7. worked like a dog last night.

_____
(Name of student)

8. thinks he/she is foxy.

_____
(Name of student)

9. has a friend who's a rat.

_____
(Name of student)

10. has lots of friends who are turkeys.

_____
(Name of student)

11. was cool as a cucumber the last time he/she went to the dentist.

_____
(Name of student)

12. wants to be the top banana.

_____
(Name of student)

13. has lots of friends who are nuts.

_____
(Name of student)

14. has a parent who's a smart cookie.

_____
(Name of student)

15. has a parent who's a peach.

_____
(Name of student)

16. thinks learning to sing is as easy as pie.

_____
(Name of student)

17. bought something last week that was a lemon.

_____
(Name of student)

18. doesn't want to bring home the bacon.

_____
(Name of student)

19. feels blue today, but doesn't know why.

_____
(Name of student)

20. goes dancing once in a blue moon.

_____
(Name of student)

21. is in the red.

_____
(Name of student)

22. is in the black.

_____
(Name of student)

23. is tickled pink about his/her progress in English.

_____
(Name of student)

24. has a sister or brother who has a swollen head.

_____
(Name of student)

25. likes to be tightfisted.

_____
(Name of student)

26. had to lend someone an ear last night.

_____
(Name of student)

27. put their foot in their mouth last week.

_____
(Name of student)

28. is extremely hotheaded.

_____
(Name of student)

29. keeps everyone at arm's length.

_____
(Name of student)

30. ran around a lot last night.

_____
(Name of student)

31. has a bottle of toilet water.

_____
(Name of student)

32. is very high about something today.

_____
(Name of student)

Answer Key

Matching Idioms

Unit 1
1. e   2. c   3. b   4. d   5. a

Unit 2
1. d   2. e   3. b   4. a   5. c

Unit 3
1. d   2. e   3. b   4. c   5. a

Unit 4
1. c   2. d   3. b   4. e   5. a

Unit 5
1. d   2. a   3. b   4. e   5. c

Unit 6
1. b   2. d   3. e   4. c   5. a

Unit 7
1. e   2. c   3. d   4. b   5. a

Unit 8
1. d   2. b   3. e   4. c   5. a

Unit 9
1. c   2. d   3. b   4. a   5. e

Index of Expressions

Notes

Notes

Notes

Notes

Notes

Notes

Notes

Notes